a Slimming World
Christmas

contents

a *Christmas* to remember

It's Christmastime and, as the carollers sing, 'tis the season to be jolly. As a Slimming World member, you'll know that this time of year really can be… jolly delicious, jolly satisfying, jolly sociable and jolly slimming too!

Because Food Optimising puts the focus firmly on everyday foods – foods that are naturally low in calories and naturally high in filling power – your seasonal spread can be sumptuous and low-Syn. All the traditional favourites fit perfectly – including prawn cocktail and terrines, roast turkey and all the trimmings… even Christmas pud and mulled wine!

And if you'd rather spend the day with your loved ones than your cooker, we've flagged starters, mains and desserts that you can make as part of a 'big day' menu in just one hour… your family will wonder just how you've done it!

Even though Christmas is just one day, it has a habit of lasting for the whole of December. And that's why *A Slimming World Christmas* is also bursting with festive bakes, cocktails, home-made gift ideas and a host of party nibbles, not to mention tasty ideas for leftovers including Christmas curry and brilliant 'bauble and squeak' cakes!

Paired with the care, friendship and shared ideas that you'll discover during IMAGE Therapy each week during the run-up to this special holiday, you'll have everything you need to make your Christmas weight loss wishes come true!

*Wishing you a
very merry Christmas…
and a slimmer New Year!*

make a three-course Christmas menu in just one hour

1 hour menu!

If you're the cook in your household, we have an early Christmas present for you… a fabulous three-course menu that's ready in super-quick time (we won't tell if you don't) – leaving you free to enjoy this special time with your family and friends.

Choose your favourites from these sensational starters, mains and desserts. Mix and match to your heart's content – whatever you go for, your three-course feast will be ready to eat in just 60 minutes!

When you're ready to cook, flick to the recipe for your chosen main course. You'll spot that the tinted boxes give guidance on when to start your other two speedy courses. All of these delicious dishes work on their own too, so you can enjoy them whether you're cooking one, two or all three courses.

1 Pick a starter

Deluxe prawn cocktail

page 12

Chicory and pear salad with blue cheese dressing

V (if the cheese is vegetarian)

page 18

Christmas salad **V**

page 26

2 Choose your **main course**

Turkey dinner at the double

page 34

Roast halibut with caper sauce

page 46

Jewelled pilaf **Ⓥ**

page 52

3 ...and don't forget **dessert**

Cherry Christmas trifles **Ⓥ**

page 78

Tropical fruit salad
with rum cream **Ⓥ**

page 83

Boozy fruit brûlées **Ⓥ**

page 88

serve up a
stress-free
Christmas!

wish upon a starter...

Serve up our stylish starters and you'll make everyone's Christmas wishes come true!

luxury
mushroom soup

serves 4

each serving is:

1½ **Syns** on Extra Easy

1½ **Syns** on Green

1½ **Syns** on Original

 (without the fromage frais)

Ⓥ

ready in 45 minutes

....

low calorie cooking spray

2 onions, finely chopped

4 garlic cloves, thinly sliced

1 tsp fresh thyme leaves

1 tsp finely chopped
fresh rosemary

400g mixed mushrooms,
thinly sliced

1.5 litres boiling vegetable stock

100ml dry sherry

salt and freshly ground
black pepper

fat free natural fromage frais,
to serve

1 tbsp finely chopped fresh
tarragon, plus sprigs to garnish

1 tbsp finely chopped
fresh parsley, to garnish

Our show-off soup makes the most of the rich,
earthy flavour of mushrooms, with a big glug of
sherry added for extra festive cheer!

Spray a large non-stick saucepan with low calorie cooking spray, add
the onions, garlic, thyme and rosemary and stir-fry over a medium heat
for 10 minutes or until the onions have softened.

Stir in all but a few of the mushrooms and cook over a high heat for a further
2 minutes. Add the stock and sherry and bring to the boil, then turn the heat
to low and simmer for 15 minutes. Season to taste and whizz with a stick
blender until smooth.

Meanwhile, lightly spray a non-stick frying pan with low calorie cooking
spray and place over a medium heat. Sauté the remaining mushrooms for
8-10 minutes or until nicely browned.

Spoon the soup into bowls, add a dollop of fromage frais and scatter
over the chopped tarragon and parsley. Garnish with the sautéed
mushrooms and tarragon sprigs to serve.

1 hour menu!

see page 6

deluxe prawn cocktail

serves 4

each serving is:

2½ Syns on Extra Easy

2½ Syns on Original

8½ Syns on Green

ready in 15 minutes

....

6 level tbsp extra-light mayonnaise

2 level tbsp tomato ketchup

2 tsp Worcestershire sauce

2 level tsp creamed horseradish

a few drops of Tabasco sauce

1 tbsp lemon juice

salt and freshly ground black pepper

500g cooked and peeled king prawns

Little Gem lettuces leaves

1 tsp smoked paprika, to garnish

fresh dill sprigs, to garnish

lime wedges, to serve

Take your guests' tastebuds on a trip down memory lane with our stylish version of the retro classic.

Mix the mayonnaise, ketchup, Worcestershire sauce, horseradish, Tabasco and lemon juice together in a large bowl. Season to taste and stir in the prawns.

Divide the Little Gem leaves between four cocktail glasses or small bowls and spoon in the prawns.

Sprinkle with a little smoked paprika, garnish with dill sprigs and serve with lime wedges to squeeze over.

chicken and ham terrine

serves 8

each serving is:

Free on Extra Easy

Free on Original

10½ Syns on Green

ready in 2 hours 20 minutes,
plus cooling and chilling

....

8 skinless and boneless chicken
thighs, roughly chopped

bunch of spring onions,
finely chopped

finely grated zest of
1 unwaxed lemon

1 egg, beaten

1 garlic clove, crushed

1 tsp crushed pink peppercorns,
plus whole pink peppercorns
to garnish

2 juniper berries, crushed

1 tbsp cognac or brandy

large handful of finely chopped
fresh parsley

small handful of finely chopped
fresh tarragon, plus sprigs
to garnish

salt and freshly ground
black pepper

600g canned lean ham, cubed

This easy terrine is packed with irresistible flavours and it's so handy because you make it in advance, saving time on the big day.

Preheat the oven to 150°C/Fan 130°C/Gas 2.

Place the chicken in a food processor and blend until fairly smooth. Transfer to a bowl and add the spring onions, lemon zest, egg, garlic, peppercorns, juniper berries, cognac or brandy, parsley and tarragon. Season and mix well.

Spoon half the mixture into an ovenproof terrine or loaf tin and scatter over the ham. Spoon the remaining chicken mixture over the ham and level with the back of a spoon.

Place the terrine or loaf tin in a roasting tin and pour in enough hot water to come halfway up the side of the terrine or loaf tin. Bake for 2 hours or until the terrine slightly shrinks away from the side of the tin. Cool, then cover with foil and weigh the top down with weights or cans. Chill for 24 hours.

When you're ready to eat, turn out the terrine on to a board. Scatter over the pink peppercorns and tarragon sprigs and slice thickly. This is delicious with a crisp salad and redcurrant sauce (2 Syns per level tablespoon).

seared scallops
with lime and chilli

Garlic, chilli and lime add a big hit of flavour to the meaty texture of scallops, and serving them in their shells really makes this a starter to remember.

Spray the scallops with low calorie cooking spray.

Heat a large non-stick frying pan over a medium-high heat. When the pan is hot, add the scallops and cook for about 1 minute until golden, then flip them over and sprinkle over the garlic and chilli. Cook for another 1-2 minutes then add the lime juice.

Put the scallops back into half-shells, spoon over any garlic and chilli left in the pan and scatter over the coriander. Season to taste and serve hot with lime wedges.

The orange part of the scallop is the coral (or roe). It's delicious, though you can remove it if you like. If you can't find any fresh scallops, the frozen kind are tasty too. Thaw completely before cooking – you'll need about 100g per person.

serves 4

each serving is:

Free on Extra Easy

Free on Original

1½ Syns on Green

ready in 15 minutes

....

8 large fresh scallops, shells separated and washed

low calorie cooking spray

3 garlic cloves, finely chopped

1 red chilli, deseeded and finely chopped

juice of 1 large lime, plus wedges to serve

small handful of finely chopped fresh coriander, to garnish

salt and freshly ground black pepper

1 hour menu!

see page 6

chicory and pear salad
with blue cheese dressing

serves 4

each serving is:

3 Syns on Extra Easy

3 Syns on Green

3 Syns on Original

Ⓥ (if the cheese is vegetarian)

ready in 10 minutes

....

4 heads of green or red chicory

small bag of mixed salad leaves

2 ripe pears

juice of 1 lemon

50g red and green seedless
grapes, halved

salt and freshly ground
black pepper

for the dressing

60g creamy blue cheese, such as
Stilton or Dolcelatte, diced

150g fat free natural fromage frais

2 tbsp white wine vinegar

a pinch of sweetener

Blue cheese is one of the classic Christmas foods and a salad dressing is a great way to enjoy it without adding loads of Syns.

Discard the outer leaves of the chicory and separate the rest of the leaves. Wash and dry the chicory leaves and put them in a bowl with the salad leaves.

Core the pears, cut them into thin wedges and toss in a bowl with the lemon juice to stop them going brown. Add to the chicory along with the grapes.

Put all the dressing ingredients in a bowl, reserving a little of the cheese. Whisk until smooth and drizzle over the salad, then season to taste and scatter over the reserved cheese to serve.

gravlax

This classic Scandinavian starter is a brilliant way to serve salmon. The fish is cured in a marinade of salt, pepper and sugar rather than cooked, giving a fabulous freshness to every mouthful.

Check that all the small pin bones have been removed from the salmon by rubbing your fingers up and down it. Remove any bones you find with tweezers.

Put the salmon fillet into a large dish. Mix the sea salt, pepper and sugar together and rub all over the salmon. Finely chop most of the dill and sprinkle over the salmon. Cover the dish loosely with cling film, put a wooden board or a plate on top of the wrapped salmon and weigh down with weights or heavy cans. Chill for 48 hours.

Mix all the sauce ingredients together in a bowl and chill until needed.

Scrape away and discard the salmon's salty marinade. Pat dry with kitchen paper, finely chop the remaining dill and scatter over the fish. Slice the salmon very thinly on the diagonal and arrange the slices on plates. Serve with the sauce and lemon wedges, if you like.

Gravlax will keep for up to a week in the fridge.

serves 8

each serving is:

½ **Syn** on Extra Easy

½ **Syn** on Original

8½ **Syns** on Green

ready in 20 minutes,
plus 2 days' chilling

....

700g loin fillet of salmon,
skin and bones removed

3 tbsp coarsely ground sea salt

1 tbsp freshly ground
black pepper

1 level tbsp caster sugar

large handful of fresh dill

lemon wedges, to serve (optional)

for the mustard and dill sauce

200g fat free natural yogurt

1 level tsp Dijon mustard

small handful of fresh dill

salt and freshly ground
black pepper

stuffed portobello mushrooms

serves 4 (makes 8)

each serving is:

Free on Extra Easy

Free on Green

Free on Original

ready in 35 minutes

⋯⋯⋯⋯⋯⋯⋯⋯⋯⋯⋯⋯⋯⋯⋯⋯

8 large portobello mushrooms

low calorie cooking spray

1 small onion, finely chopped

4 garlic cloves, crushed

small bag of baby leaf spinach, roughly chopped

3 bottled roasted red peppers in brine, rinsed and roughly chopped

1 tsp dried chilli flakes

1 tsp finely chopped fresh rosemary, plus sprigs to garnish

4 tbsp low fat natural cottage cheese

salt and freshly ground black pepper

Giant mushrooms are filled with cottage cheese, spinach and roasted red peppers to make a sensational vegetarian starter.

Preheat the oven to 200°C/Fan 180°C/Gas 6.

Wipe the mushrooms clean with damp kitchen paper, then carefully remove and dice the stems.

Spray a large non-stick frying pan with low calorie cooking spray and place over a medium heat. When hot, add the mushroom stems, onion and garlic and cook for 5 minutes. Add the spinach, peppers, chilli and rosemary and stir-fry for 3 minutes.

Take the pan off the heat and add the cottage cheese. Season to taste and stir well.

Fill the mushroom caps with the spinach mixture, spread them out on a non-stick baking tray and bake for 15-20 minutes.

Arrange the mushrooms on a platter and garnish with rosemary sprigs to serve.

carrot and beetroot soup

serves 6

each serving is:

Free on Extra Easy

Free on Green

Free on Original

 (without the fromage frais)

𝒱

ready in 1½ hours

....

low calorie cooking spray

450g beetroot, peeled and diced

3 large carrots, peeled and diced

2 onions, chopped

1 tsp sweetener

1 bay leaf

1.8 litres boiling vegetable stock

fat free natural fromage frais, to serve

a few fresh chives, some finely chopped, to serve

The rich colour and satisfying flavour of this elegant wintry soup make it the perfect choice for Christmas Day.

Spray a large non-stick saucepan with low calorie cooking spray and place over a medium heat. Add the beetroot, carrots and onions and cook for 8-10 minutes or until slightly softened.

Add the sweetener, bay leaf and stock, turn the heat to low and simmer for 1 hour or until softened.

Discard the bay leaf and reserve a few beetroot dice for garnishing, then blitz the rest of the mixture with a stick blender until almost smooth.

Ladle the soup into bowls, add a dollop of fromage frais to each one and scatter over the reserved beetroot and the chives to serve.

1 hour menu!

see page 6

Christmas salad

serves 4

each serving is:

½ **Syn** on Extra Easy

½ **Syn** on Green

½ **Syn** on Original

ready in 15 minutes

....

¼ red cabbage, finely shredded

¼ green cabbage, finely shredded

1 carrot, peeled and cut into thin matchsticks

1 orange, segmented

1 apple, cored and cut into matchsticks

8 black olives

salt and freshly ground black pepper

for the dressing

3 tbsp fat free vinaigrette

1 garlic clove, crushed

½ tbsp white wine vinegar

a pinch of sweetener

juice of ½ orange

This very special starter is full of colours and goodness – plus it's on the table in just 15 minutes!

Put the red and green cabbage, carrot, orange, apple and olives into a serving bowl.

Mix all the dressing ingredients together in a small bowl and drizzle over the fruit and vegetables.

Season to taste and toss well to serve.

Leave out the olives to make this seasonal salad Free. You can change the flavours by using a peach or nectarine instead of an orange, or trying pear instead of apple.

hot-smoked trout pâté

Serve up a taste of luxury with this indulgent yet very simple starter.

Spray a non-stick frying pan with low calorie cooking spray. Add most of the spring onions, reserving a few slices to garnish, and fry for 1 minute. Add the trout and cook for a further minute.

Transfer the trout and spring onions to a bowl and stir in the quark, horseradish and Tabasco. Mix together until well combined.

Divide the pâté between ramekins or small serving bowls and garnish with dill sprigs, peppercorns and the remaining spring onions. Grind over a little black pepper and serve with your favourite vegetable crudités.

serves 12

each serving is:

Free on Extra Easy

Free on Original

2½ Syns on Green

ready in 15 minutes

....

low calorie cooking spray

bunch of spring onions, finely sliced

450g hot-smoked trout, finely chopped

250g quark

1 level tsp creamed horseradish

a dash of Tabasco sauce

a few sprigs of fresh dill, to garnish

pink peppercorns, to garnish

freshly ground black pepper

the
main attraction

Whether you want a traditional turkey, a meat-free
marvel or some festive fish, you'll find a recipe here to
make your Christmas unforgettable.

roast turkey

serves 6

each serving is:

Free on Extra Easy

Free on Original

26 Syns on Green

ready in 4 hours 15 minutes, plus chilling and resting

....

4kg oven-ready turkey

small handful of finely chopped fresh parsley

4 tbsp dried mixed herbs

4 unwaxed lemons

low calorie cooking spray

1 onion, halved

2 garlic bulbs, unpeeled

a small handful of sage leaves

bay leaves, to garnish

for the stuffing balls

small handful of chopped fresh sage

small handful of chopped fresh parsley

1 egg, beaten

finely grated zest of ½ unwaxed lemon

350g lean pork mince (5% fat or less)

salt and freshly ground black pepper

6 lean bacon rashers, visible fat removed

Push the boat out this Christmas with our sensational version of the season's essential dish. A 4kg turkey is great for six people – go for a larger bird if you're feeding more or want lots of leftovers!

First make the stuffing ball mix. Put the chopped herbs, egg, lemon zest and pork in a bowl and season to taste. Using your fingers, mix the ingredients until well combined. Cover and chill for 3-4 hours (or overnight if time permits).

Preheat the oven to 180°C/Fan 160°C/Gas 4.

Calculate the cooking time of the turkey at 45 minutes per 1kg plus 20 minutes (so a 4kg bird would take 3 hours 20 minutes). Place the turkey in a non-stick roasting tin and sprinkle over the parsley and mixed herbs plus the zest and juice of two lemons. Season and spray with low calorie cooking spray. Halve the remaining lemons and stuff them into the turkey's body cavity along with the onion, garlic and sage. Tie the legs together with kitchen string.

Cover with foil and roast in the oven, basting with the juices in the tin every hour or so. Increase the temperature to 200°C/Fan 180°C/Gas 6 and remove the foil for the final 30 minutes. Remove the turkey from the oven, cover with a 'tent' of foil and leave to rest for up to 2 hours.

Meanwhile, make the stuffing balls. Divide the stuffing ball mixture into 12 bite-sized balls. Halve each bacon rasher lengthways and use each piece to wrap up a stuffing ball. Place them seam side down in a non-stick roasting tin and roast in an oven preheated to 200°C/Fan 180°C/Gas 6 for 35 minutes or until cooked through.

Remove the skin and any visible fat from the turkey and place the bird on a serving platter. Garnish with bay leaves and serve with the stuffing balls and all the trimmings!

*If you have any turkey meat left over,
take a look at our quick Christmas curry
on page 104 and our turkey risotto on page 106.*

turkey dinner *at the double*

serves 4

each serving is:

1 Syn on Extra Easy

14 Syns on Original

16½ Syns on Green

ready in 50 minutes

························

1kg baby new potatoes,
washed or scrubbed

low calorie cooking spray

300g prepared butternut
squash chunks

4 large parsnips, peeled and
cut into chunks

salt and freshly ground
black pepper

1 tbsp dried mixed herbs

8 turkey breast steaks

4 Sainsbury's Be Good to Yourself
Cumberland Sausages,
Less Than 3% Fat*

4 lean bacon rashers,
visible fat removed

small handful of finely chopped
fresh parsley, to garnish

*We've counted 1 Syn each for the
sausages on Extra Easy and Original,
and 4 Syns on Green but Syn values
for branded foods can change. You
can find the latest information online at
www.slimmingworld.com/lifelineonline*

Our short-cut version features all the bits you love
and will be on the table in less than an hour, giving
you so much more time to enjoy the big day.

Preheat the oven to 200°C/Fan 180°C/Gas 6.

Cook the potatoes in a pan of lightly salted boiling water for 8-10 minutes
or until just starting to soften, then drain well and tip into a roasting tin
sprayed with low calorie cooking spray.

Meanwhile, cook the squash and parsnips in a pan of lightly salted boiling
water for 8-10 minutes or until just starting to soften, then drain well and
tip into another roasting tin sprayed with low calorie cooking spray.
Sprinkle both tins with salt and the mixed herbs and roast for 30 minutes
or until golden.

Preheat the grill to medium-high.

Season the turkey breast steaks, spray with low calorie cooking spray
and roast on top of the vegetables for the last 20 minutes.

Wrap the sausages in the bacon to make pigs in blankets and grill for
20 minutes, turning now and then.

*If you're making this dish for one of our one-hour Christmas menus
(see page 6), make your dessert while the meat and vegetables are
cooking and chill until you're ready to serve.*

Keep everything warm in a low oven.

*If you're following the one-hour menu (see page 6), make your starter
and serve it straight away.*

Put the turkey steaks on to plates with the pigs in blankets and roast
vegetables and scatter over the parsley to serve.

*If you'd like gravy with your turkey dinner,
make up some gravy granules according to
the packet instructions. Using four level teaspoons
of dried granules adds 1 Syn per serving.*

roast beef
with a mustard crust

serves 6

each serving is:

Free on Extra Easy

Free on Original

16 Syns on Green

ready in 2 hours, plus resting

....

1.5kg sirloin of beef,
visible fat removed

1 tbsp English mustard powder
mixed with 1 tbsp water

4 tbsp tomato purée

6-8 tbsp mixed peppercorns,
crushed

rosemary sprigs, to garnish
(optional)

A little mustard and tomato purée takes beef to another level and this oh-so-simple roast will be the star of any festive table.

Preheat the oven to 190°C/Fan 170°C/Gas 5.

Put the beef in a roasting tin. Mix the made-up mustard and tomato purée and spread over the joint. Sprinkle over the peppercorns to form an even crust.

Put the joint in the oven and cook to your liking (22 minutes per 500g plus an extra 20 minutes for rare; 28 minutes per 500g plus an extra 25 minutes for medium; and 33 minutes per 500g plus an extra 30 minutes for well done – so a 1.5kg joint cooked to medium needs 1 hour 50 minutes). Baste occasionally with the meat juices while roasting, and turn halfway through the cooking time.

Once cooked, put the beef on a serving dish, cover loosely with foil and leave to rest for 15-20 minutes. Garnish with rosemary sprigs if you like, then carve and serve with your favourite potatoes and vegetables.

If you have any beef left over, try our fantastic chilli noodles on page 109.

festive pork hotpot

Bring out the succulent pleasures of pork with this simple and colourful main course.

Preheat the oven to 160°C/Fan 140°C/Gas 3.

Spray a large non-stick ovenproof casserole pan with low calorie cooking spray and place over a high heat. In batches, add the pork and cook for 3-4 minutes or until lightly browned. Transfer to a plate and keep warm.

Turn the heat to medium, add the onions to the same pan and stir-fry for 10 minutes or until softened, adding a little water if they start to stick. Stir in the carrots and cook for 1 minute, then add the flour and cook for 1 minute to soak up the juices. Gradually add the stock, stir until smooth and season to taste.

Stir in the peppers, cabbage and pork and add the rosemary sprigs. Overlap the potato slices on top and spray with low calorie cooking spray. Cover with a tight-fitting lid and cook near the top of the oven for 1 hour.

Remove the lid, lightly spray with low calorie cooking spray and cook uncovered for 30-40 minutes or until the potatoes are tender and golden.

Scatter over the parsley and serve hot.

serves 6

each serving is:

½ Syn on Extra Easy

5½ Syns on Original

11 Syns on Green

ready in 2 hours

....

low calorie cooking spray

1kg lean pork fillet, visible fat removed, cut into bite-sized pieces

3 onions, roughly chopped

2 large carrots, roughly chopped

1 level tbsp plain flour

600ml boiling chicken stock

salt and freshly ground black pepper

2 red peppers, deseeded and quartered

2 yellow peppers, deseeded and quartered

¼ green cabbage, thickly sliced

2 rosemary sprigs

800g large potatoes, peeled and cut into thick slices

small handful of roughly chopped fresh parsley, to garnish

duck breasts
with cherry sauce

serves 4

each serving is:

2 Syns on Extra Easy

2 Syns on Original

15½ Syns on Green

ready in 30 minutes

....

low calorie cooking spray

salt and freshly ground
black pepper

4 duck breasts, skinned,
visible fat removed

for the cherry sauce

2 red onions, finely chopped

100g cherries, pitted
(or use frozen cherries, thawed)

2 tbsp red wine vinegar

1 tsp coriander seeds, crushed

1 level tbsp redcurrant jelly

1-2 tbsp sweetener

150ml boiling chicken stock

1 level tbsp chicken gravy granules

The sweetness of cherry sauce makes it a classic partner for rich duck breasts in this simple seasonal treat.

Preheat the grill to medium-hot.

Spray the grill rack with low calorie cooking spray. Season the duck breasts and grill until cooked to your liking (3-4 minutes each side for rare; 4-6 minutes each side for medium; and 6-8 minutes each side for well done).

While the duck is cooking, make the sauce. Spray a large non-stick frying pan with low calorie cooking spray and place over a medium heat. Add the onions and cherries and stir-fry for 5 minutes. Add the remaining sauce ingredients and cook for 10 minutes or until thickened.

Slice the duck breasts, divide between plates and serve hot with the cherry sauce and your favourite potatoes and vegetables.

spiced gammon
with plum sauce

serves 8

each serving is:

2 Syns on Extra Easy

2 Syns on Original

21½ Syns on Green

ready in 3 hours,
plus cooling and standing

....

2.25kg boneless unsmoked
gammon joint

1 celery stick, halved

1 onion, halved

2 bay leaves

1 cinnamon stick, broken

2 tbsp whole cloves

4 level tbsp reduced
sugar marmalade

for the plum sauce

1 red onion, roughly chopped

3 garlic cloves, crushed

1cm piece of root ginger,
peeled and grated

600g plums, pitted and
roughly chopped

2 tbsp dark soy sauce

¼ tsp finely ground star anise

2 tsp sweetener (or to taste)

Juicy gammon is always a treat and
our Asian-inspired plum sauce is a truly
mouth-watering accompaniment.

Rinse the gammon joint, pat dry with kitchen paper and place in a large
saucepan. Add the celery, onion, bay leaves, cinnamon stick and 1 tsp of
the cloves. Pour in enough cold water to cover the joint completely and
bring to the boil – this will take about 15 minutes. Cover the pan and
simmer for 1 hour 45 minutes, topping up with boiling water as necessary.
Drain the gammon, discarding the vegetables and spices, and set aside
for 15 minutes.

Preheat the oven to 200°C/Fan 180°C/Gas 6.

Put the marmalade in a pan over a low heat to soften.

Slice off the rind from the gammon, leaving a thin layer of white fat, and
place the joint in a roasting tin. Score the fat with a criss-cross pattern,
and push a clove into each of the diamonds.

Brush the marmalade over the fat and roast for 30-35 minutes until
tender and hot. Drain well, transfer to a serving plate, cover with foil
and leave to stand for 20 minutes.

Meanwhile, put all the ingredients for the sauce into a heavy-based
saucepan with 100ml of water and bring to the boil over a high heat.
Reduce the heat to low and simmer for 25-30 minutes, stirring occasionally,
or until the plums have broken down. Remove from the heat and keep warm
(you can also serve this sauce at room temperature).

Remove any visible fat from the gammon (or if you can't resist, 100g meat
and fat is 5½ Syns). This is delicious served hot with the plum sauce and
your favourite potatoes and vegetables.

If you have any gammon left over,
try our fantastic bake on page 111.

poached salmon
with lemon and lime mayo

serves 10

each serving is:

1 Syn on Extra Easy

1 Syn on Original

13 Syns on Green

ready in 1 hour, plus cooling

....

150ml dry white wine

1 onion, sliced

1 carrot, peeled and sliced

1 celery stick, sliced

1 ready-made bouquet garni
(bay leaf, parsley and thyme)

1.3kg skinless and boneless
side of salmon

½ cucumber, thinly sliced, to garnish

1 lime, thinly sliced, to garnish

fresh dill sprigs, to garnish

for the lemon and lime mayo

finely grated zest and juice of
1 unwaxed lime

finely grated zest and juice of
1 unwaxed lemon

6 tbsp extra-light mayonnaise

250g low fat natural cottage cheese

200g quark

a pinch of sweetener (or to taste)

1 red chilli, deseeded and finely
chopped

small handful of finely chopped
fresh dill

salt and freshly ground
black pepper

Salmon is the perfect fish for Christmas and the soft flakes from this generous side of salmon will keep everyone happy.

Put the wine, onion, carrot, celery and bouquet garni plus 1 litre of water in a fish kettle or saucepan large enough to hold the salmon. Bring to the boil over a high heat, then lower the heat and simmer gently for 20 minutes.

Add the salmon to the pan, cover with a lid and simmer gently for 15 minutes. Turn off the heat and leave the salmon and cooking liquid to cool in the pan.

Meanwhile, put all the ingredients for the mayonnaise in a food processor or blender, reserving a little of the zest, chilli and dill to garnish the mayo before serving. Season to taste and blend until smooth. Chill until ready to serve (it will keep in the fridge for up to 3 days).

Remove the salmon from the pan and carefully remove any small bones you can see with tweezers. Arrange the salmon on a large platter and garnish with the cucumber, lime and dill sprigs.

Scatter the reserved zest, chilli and dill over the mayonnaise and serve with the salmon and your favourite potatoes and vegetables.

If you have any salmon left over,
try our tasty kedgeree on page 112.

1 hour menu!

see page 6

roast halibut with caper sauce

serves 4

each serving is:

½ **Syn** on Extra Easy

8½ **Syns** on Original

10½ **Syns** on Green

ready in 30 minutes

....

1kg baby new potatoes, washed or scrubbed

salt and freshly ground black pepper

small handful of chopped fresh dill, plus sprigs to garnish

4 halibut steaks or fillets (about 200g each)

low calorie cooking spray

600g asparagus, trimmed

lemon wedges, to serve

for the caper sauce

300ml boiling fish or vegetable stock

2 tbsp capers, rinsed and drained

2 large shallots, finely chopped

1 garlic clove, crushed

1 level tsp gravy granules

If you love fish, the firm texture and delicate flavour of halibut makes it a sensational choice for an upmarket (and quick) Christmas dinner.

Preheat the oven to 220°C/Fan 200°C/Gas 7.

If you're making this dish for one of our one-hour Christmas menus (see page 6), make your dessert and starter first and chill or set aside until you're ready to serve.

Cook the potatoes in a large saucepan of lightly salted boiling water for 12-15 minutes. Drain, return to the saucepan and lightly crush with the back of a fork. Season to taste and stir in the dill.

Meanwhile, place the fish on a non-stick baking tray, season to taste, spray with low calorie cooking spray and bake for 10-12 minutes or until just cooked through.

Blanch the asparagus in a pan of lightly salted boiling water for 3-4 minutes then drain and season to taste.

Make the sauce by putting the stock, capers, shallots and garlic in a saucepan and bringing to the boil. Add the gravy granules, stir to mix well and cook for 3-4 minutes or until thickened. Season to taste.

If you're making this for our one-hour menu, keep everything warm while you serve the starter.

Put the halibut on to warmed plates with the asparagus. Spoon over the caper sauce, garnish with dill sprigs and serve with the crushed potatoes and lemon wedges.

mediterranean vegetable filo tart

serves 6

each serving is:

2 Syns on Extra Easy

2 Syns on Green

2 Syns on Original

ready in 1 hour

....

low calorie cooking spray

2 x 45g sheets of ready-rolled filo
pastry, halved

2 courgettes, cut into chunks

1 aubergine, cut into chunks

1 onion, roughly chopped

1 red pepper, deseeded
and cut into chunks

1 yellow pepper, deseeded
and cut into chunks

200g red and yellow cherry
tomatoes, halved

2 tbsp balsamic vinegar

salt and freshly ground
black pepper

small handful of finely chopped
fresh parsley, to garnish

Fresh vegetables are gift-wrapped in crunchy filo pastry for this seriously more-ish festive delight!

Preheat the oven to 200°C/Fan 180°C/Gas 6.

Spray a 30 x 20cm baking dish with a little low calorie cooking spray. Line the dish with the filo pastry, gently scrunching any pastry that goes over the sides. Spray with a little more low calorie cooking spray.

Spray a non-stick saucepan with low calorie cooking spray and place over a medium heat. Add the courgettes, aubergine, onion and peppers and cook for 6 minutes. Add the tomatoes and vinegar and cook for a further 3 minutes. Season to taste and spoon into the pastry.

Bake for 20-25 minutes or until the pastry is crisp and golden. Sprinkle over the parsley and serve hot with salad or some of our delicious trimmings (see next chapter)!

Christmas vegetable terrine

Say goodbye to high-Syn 70s-style nut roasts with our spectacular veggie terrine. It's packed with fresh veg and has a scattering of crunchy nuts for old time's sake!

Preheat the oven to 160°C/Fan 140°C/Gas 3.

Line a terrine tin or large loaf tin with a double layer of cling film and place in a deep roasting tin.

Cook the carrots and green beans in a large saucepan of lightly salted boiling water for 3-4 minutes, then add the courgette and cook for another 3-4 minutes. Drain the vegetables and run under cold water to stop them cooking.

Meanwhile, beat the eggs with the quark until well blended, stir in the tarragon and season to taste. Pour enough egg mixture into the terrine or loaf tin to come about 1cm up the side.

Add layers of carrots, green beans, courgette and peppers to the terrine tin then pour the remaining egg mixture over the top. Cover with foil and pour boiling water into the roasting tin to come halfway up the sides of the roasting tin. Put the roasting tin in the oven and bake for around 1 hour 15 minutes or until set.

Remove the terrine or loaf tin from the roasting tin and leave to cool completely. Cover and chill for 6-8 hours.

When you're ready to eat, turn out the terrine from its tin and take off the cling film.

Dry-fry the nuts for a minute or two to give a nice colour then scatter them over the terrine. Garnish with the tarragon sprigs, cut into thick slices and serve with your favourite potatoes and vegetables.

Leave out the nuts to make this tasty terrine Free on all choices!

serves 8

each serving is:

1 Syn on Extra Easy

1 Syn on Green

1 Syn on Original

ready in 1½ hours, plus cooling and chilling

2 carrots, peeled and sliced into matchsticks

200g green beans, trimmed

1 large courgette, sliced into matchsticks

8 large eggs

100g quark

small handful of finely chopped fresh tarragon, plus sprigs to garnish

salt and freshly ground black pepper

3 bottled roasted red peppers in brine, drained and thickly sliced

20g roughly chopped toasted cashew nuts or hazelnuts

1 hour menu!
see page 6

jewelled pilaf

serves 4

each serving is:

Free on Extra Easy

Free on Green

21 Syns on Original

ready in 35 minutes,
plus standing

....

1 tbsp saffron threads

400g dried basmati or
long-grain rice

low calorie cooking spray

3 shallots, finely chopped

2 garlic cloves, finely chopped

6 cardamom pods, lightly bruised

2 cloves

2 cinnamon sticks

1 tsp turmeric

6 black peppercorns

2 tsp cumin seeds

2 carrots, peeled and diced

600ml boiling vegetable stock

salt and freshly ground
black pepper

200g soya beans, thawed if frozen

100g pomegranate seeds

large handful of finely chopped
fresh dill

The glittering colours and fabulous flavours make pilaf a great speedy vegetarian choice – plus it's the rice dish of choice in the Middle East, where the Christmas story began!

Soak the saffron in 200ml of boiling water and set aside.

Rinse the rice in cold running water and leave to drain until needed.

If you're making this dish for one of our one-hour Christmas menus (see page 6), make your dessert and chill until you're ready to serve.

Spray a heavy-based saucepan with low calorie cooking spray and place over a medium heat. Add the shallots and garlic and stir-fry for 3-4 minutes. Add the rice, cardamom pods, cloves, cinnamon sticks, turmeric, peppercorns, cumin seeds and carrots and stir to mix well. Add the stock and saffron mixture and season to taste. Bring to the boil over a high heat and stir in the soya beans, then cover tightly and reduce the heat to low. Cook for 15 minutes without lifting the lid.

If you're following one of our one-hour menus (see page 6), make your starter and set aside.

Remove the pilaf from the heat and leave to stand for 10-15 minutes, undisturbed.

If you're making this as part of a one-hour menu, serve the starter while the pilaf is standing.

Remove the lid from the pan (the liquid should have been completely absorbed by now). Scatter the pomegranate seeds and dill over the pilaf and serve hot.

For an even 'fruitier' pilaf, stir through 25g raisins or sultanas before serving (adds 1 Syn per serving).

all the trimmings

It's the side dishes that make Christmas meals so memorable, and ours include veg with an edge, chutneys full of cheer and all the essential sauces.

chestnut sprouts

Even sprout-haters will be tempted by this clever dish, while sprout-lovers are in for a treat!

serves 6

each serving is:

2½ **Syns** on Extra Easy

2½ **Syns** on Green

2½ **Syns** on Original

ready in 30 minutes

....

500g Brussels sprouts, trimmed

low calorie cooking spray

1 red onion, finely chopped

½ tsp fennel seeds

finely grated zest of 1 orange

½ tsp thyme leaves

170g cooked chestnuts

salt and freshly ground black pepper

Cook the sprouts in a saucepan of lightly salted boiling water for 6 minutes. Drain well.

Meanwhile, spray a non-stick frying pan with low calorie cooking spray and cook the onion, fennel seeds, orange zest and thyme for a few minutes over a high heat until the onion starts to colour.

Tip in the sprouts and the chestnuts and continue frying until the sprouts are slightly browned. Season to taste and serve hot.

maple-glazed carrots

Transform simple carrots into something irresistible with a little maple syrup.

serves 6

each serving is:

½ **Syn** on Extra Easy

½ **Syn** on Green

½ **Syn** on Original

ready in 30 minutes

....

800g carrots, peeled and cut into batons

1 level tbsp maple syrup

1 tbsp caraway seeds

salt and freshly ground black pepper

Put the carrots in a wide, shallow pan with the maple syrup and caraway seeds. Season to taste and add enough water to cover the carrots.

Bring to a simmer over a medium heat then cover and cook until the carrots are almost tender (about 10-15 minutes). Turn the heat to high, remove the lid and cook until all the liquid has evaporated and the carrots are glazed. Serve hot.

potato and celeriac mash

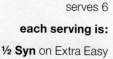

serves 6

each serving is:

½ **Syn** on Extra Easy

½ **Syn** on Green

2½ **Syns** on Original

❄ Ⓥ

ready in 40 minutes

....

900g celeriac, peeled and cut into cubes

2 large potatoes, peeled and chopped

2 garlic cloves, crushed

100ml skimmed milk

salt and freshly ground black pepper

freshly grated nutmeg

bay leaves, to garnish

Give mash a flavour boost by mixing it with celeriac and a little freshly grated nutmeg.

Place the celeriac and potatoes in a large saucepan of lightly salted boiling water and simmer for 20 minutes or until tender. Drain well and return to the pan.

Add the garlic and milk, season to taste and mash well. Sprinkle with nutmeg, garnish with bay leaves and serve hot.

Try mashing potatoes with other root veg too: swede, parsnips or sweet potatoes will all be delicious.

hedgehog potatoes

Roast spuds are a must at Christmas and our cute and crispy hedgehog potatoes will make your feast extra special.

Preheat the oven to 200°C/Fan 180°C/Gas 6.

Cut deep slices into the potatoes at regular intervals, taking care not to cut right through.

Place on a baking tray and spray with low calorie cooking spray. Tuck rosemary sprigs into a few of the slices and season to taste.

Roast in the oven for 1 hour or until cooked through. Garnish with extra rosemary sprigs to serve.

You could use any size of potatoes for this dish. If you prefer new potatoes, roast for around 40-45 minutes instead.

serves 6

each serving is:

Free on Extra Easy

Free on Green

8½ Syns on Original

ready in 1 hour 10 minutes

....

6 baking potatoes, scrubbed

low calorie cooking spray

rosemary sprigs, plus extra to garnish

sea salt and freshly ground black pepper

red onion nests

serves 6

each serving is:

Free on Extra Easy

Free on Green

Free on Original

ready in 1½ hours

....

6 red onions

low calorie cooking spray

1 tbsp balsamic vinegar

salt and freshly ground
black pepper

1 celery stick, finely chopped

1 garlic clove, crushed

85g fresh cranberries

small handful of roughly chopped
fresh parsley

These beautiful stuffed onions will bring some stunning colours and flavours to your table.

Preheat the oven to 180°C/Fan 160°C/Gas 4.

Peel the onions (keeping the base intact) and cut each one in half horizontally. Remove and reserve several layers from the centre of each onion. Arrange the onion halves in an ovenproof dish and spray with low calorie cooking spray.

Whisk together half of the vinegar and some seasoning and drizzle over the onions. Cover with foil and bake for 15-20 minutes or until the onions are almost tender.

Place a non-stick frying pan over a medium heat and spray with low calorie cooking spray. Chop the reserved onion and add to the pan along with the celery. Cook for about 5 minutes then add the garlic and cranberries and cook gently for 6-8 minutes. Remove from the heat and season to taste.

Spoon the mixture into the onion shells and drizzle over the remaining vinegar. Put the stuffed onions back in the oven and bake for another 6-8 minutes. Scatter over the parsley and serve hot.

sweet vegetable roast

serves 8

each serving is:

½ **Syn** on Extra Easy

½ **Syn** on Green

½ **Syn** on Original

❅ Ⓥ

ready in 1 hour

....

1 large butternut squash, peeled and cut into chunks

450g carrots, peeled and cut into chunks

4 red peppers, halved, deseeded and cut into chunks

300g shallots, peeled and halved if large

juice of 1 large lemon

1 tbsp chopped fresh rosemary leaves, plus sprigs to garnish

1 tsp ground cinnamon

2 level tsp clear honey

salt and freshly ground black pepper

1 tbsp chopped fresh parsley, to garnish

You can't have too much choice at Christmas and these alternative vegetables are roasted to perfection in a more-ish marinade of rosemary, honey and cinnamon.

Preheat the oven to 200°C/Fan 180°C/Gas 6.

Put all of the vegetables into a large bowl.

Mix the lemon juice, rosemary, cinnamon and honey in a small bowl and stir into the vegetables to coat them well.

Spread the vegetables out in a roasting tin lined with non-stick baking parchment and season to taste. Cover with foil and cook for 20 minutes.

Remove the foil, turn the vegetables over and roast for a further 20 minutes or until tender and lightly browned. Drain off any juices, scatter over the parsley and garnish with rosemary sprigs to serve.

If you have any of your sweet vegetable roast left over, try our tasty gammon bake on page 111.

braised
red cabbage

It wouldn't be Christmas without a big bowl of red cabbage and our fab version features red onions, pink apples and festive nutmeg.

Discard any damaged outer leaves from the cabbage, slice out and discard the coarse stem and finely shred the rest.

In a large pan, layer the cabbage with the onions, seasoning with salt and pepper and sprinkling the ground nutmeg as you go.

Spoon over the red wine vinegar and cover the pan with a tight-fitting lid. Place over a very low heat and cook for about 45 minutes, stirring occasionally and making sure that the mixture doesn't dry out – add a little water if it does.

Cut the apples into quarters, remove the core, slice thinly and toss the slices in the lemon juice. Lay the apple on top of the cabbage, replace the lid and cook for a further 25 minutes or until tender. Gently mix the apples into the cabbage and add sweetener to taste.

This dish reheats well. You can cook it up to two days before serving then leave to cool, cover and chill. Reheat thoroughly in a microwave or place the cabbage in a pan with 4 tablespoons of water, bring to the boil and simmer, stirring, until heated through.

serves 8

each serving is:

1 Syn on Extra Easy

1 Syn on Green

1 Syn on Original

ready in 1½ hours

....

1 red cabbage

2 red onions, halved and finely sliced

salt and freshly ground black pepper

1 tsp freshly grated nutmeg

3 tbsp red wine vinegar

2 pink-skinned eating apples

juice of ½ lemon

sweetener, to taste

baby leeks au gratin

serves 4

each serving is:

2½ Syns on Extra Easy

2½ Syns on Original

7 Syns on Green

ready in 30 minutes

12 baby leeks

12 slices of lean ham, visible fat removed

2 level tbsp freshly grated Parmesan

for the white sauce

2 level tsp cornflour

300ml skimmed milk

3 tbsp fat free natural fromage frais

salt and freshly ground black pepper

freshly grated nutmeg

1 egg, lightly beaten

Tasty ham is wrapped around fresh baby leeks and smothered in white sauce and Parmesan to make this stylish side dish, which might just steal the show!

Cook the leeks in lightly salted boiling water for 3-4 minutes or until they are just tender. Drain thoroughly and set aside.

Meanwhile, make the white sauce. Blend the cornflour with a little of the milk. Heat the remaining milk in a saucepan and bring to the boil over a high heat. Stir in the cornflour mixture and cook over a low heat for 1-2 minutes, stirring until thickened. Remove from the heat, beat in the fromage frais and season to taste with salt, black pepper and nutmeg. Leave to cool then stir in the egg.

Preheat the grill to high.

Wrap a strip of ham around each leek and arrange the leeks in a single layer in a small ovenproof dish. Drizzle with the white sauce and scatter over the Parmesan.

Grill for 4-5 minutes or until golden and serve hot.

This dish is a great way to use up leftover Christmas ham. It also works really well with asparagus instead of leeks.

serves 6

each serving is:

1 Syn on Extra Easy

1 Syn on Green

1 Syn on Original

ready in 50 minutes, plus cooling

1kg fresh beetroot, peeled and cut into bite-sized pieces

low calorie cooking spray

2 garlic cloves, finely chopped

1 tsp ground ginger

2 tsp cumin seeds

1 tsp black mustard seeds

1 tsp ground cumin

1 tsp cinnamon

small bag of rocket leaves

small handful of finely chopped fresh coriander

1 red chilli, deseeded and finely chopped

for the coconut cream

100ml light coconut milk

200g fat free natural fromage frais

juice of 1 lime

salt and freshly ground black pepper

spiced beetroot
with coconut cream

Fragrant Indian spices and creamy coconut milk transform this vibrant vegetable into a Christmas treat.

Preheat the oven to 200°C/Fan 180°C/Gas 6.

Put the beetroot on a non-stick baking sheet and spray with low calorie cooking spray. Roast for 35-40 minutes or until the beetroot is just tender then set aside to cool.

Meanwhile, spray a large non-stick frying pan with low calorie cooking spray and place over a high heat. Add the garlic, ginger, cumin seeds, mustard seeds, ground cumin and cinnamon and stir-fry for 20-30 seconds, then remove from the heat and set aside to cool.

Make the coconut cream by whisking the coconut milk, fromage frais, lime juice and a little seasoning in a bowl.

Arrange the rocket leaves on a serving platter, top with the beetroot and drizzle over the coconut cream. Sprinkle over the spice mix and scatter over the coriander and chilli to serve.

cranberry and plum salsa

Our winter salsa is a tomato-free zone, featuring festive cranberries, plums and sherry!

Place the cranberries in a small saucepan with 6 tablespoons of water. Bring to the boil over a high heat then cover and turn the heat to low. Simmer for 5-6 minutes or until tender, then set aside to cool.

Put the plums and sherry in a bowl and mix well, then cover and chill.

When the cranberries have cooled, mix them with the plums and add sweetener to taste. Stir in the ginger, cover and chill until you're ready to eat.

Sealed well, this salsa will keep for 4-5 days in the fridge.

serves 8

each serving is:

½ **Syn** on Extra Easy

½ **Syn** on Green

½ **Syn** on Original

ready in 15 minutes, plus cooling

170g fresh cranberries

4 ripe plums,
stoned and diced

2 tbsp dry sherry

sweetener, to taste

1 tsp ground ginger

best-ever turkey gravy

Use the giblets packed inside your turkey to make a rich, tasty gravy that's remarkably low in Syns.

serves 8

each serving is:

1 Syn on Extra Easy

1 Syn on Original

2 Syns on Green

ready in 2 hours, plus soaking and cooling

....

giblets from 1 turkey

1 onion, sliced

1 carrot, peeled and sliced

1 bay leaf

a few sprigs of fresh parsley

1 level tbsp gravy granules

salt and freshly ground black pepper

1 level tbsp cranberry jelly

Soak the giblets in salted water for about 45 minutes.

Rinse the giblets and put them in a saucepan with the onion, carrot, herbs and 600ml of water. Bring to the boil and simmer for about 1½ hours. Strain and set aside to cool.

Mix the gravy granules with a little of the cold stock in a clean saucepan. Add the remaining stock and bring to the boil. Season to taste and stir in the cranberry jelly.

Simmer for 5-10 minutes and keep warm until you're ready to serve.

classic cranberry sauce

It's so easy to make your own cranberry sauce – and if you like to get ahead with your cooking, this is a great recipe to make and chill in advance.

serves 8

each serving is:

½ Syn on Extra Easy

½ Syn on Green

½ Syn on Original

ready in 20 minutes, plus cooling

....

450g fresh cranberries

sweetener, to taste

grated zest of 1 orange, plus a few thin strips to garnish

Put the cranberries in a small saucepan with a splash of water and bring to the boil over a high heat.

Reduce the heat and simmer gently for about 10 minutes. The cranberries will pop open and the sauce will become thick and pulpy. Sweeten to taste and stir in the orange zest.

Leave to cool then transfer to a serving bowl, cover and keep in the fridge until needed.

Garnish with the orange strips to serve.

spiced clementine preserve

Clementines are so Christmassy and they're sensational in this easy preserve.

Cut the clementines into thin rounds, discarding the ends, and put them in a saucepan with 600ml of water. Bring to a simmer and cook for 30-40 minutes or until tender. Lift out the clementines with a slotted spoon and set aside.

Add the sugar, vinegar and spices to the liquid in the pan and heat gently, stirring, until the sugar dissolves. Bring to the boil and boil for 10 minutes or until reduced by half.

Turn the heat to low and return the clementines to the pan. Simmer for 15 minutes, then divide the clementines between two sterilised half-litre Kilner jars (see tip, right).

Turn the heat to high and boil the liquid until it is syrupy. Pour it into the jars and cool. Cover with a waxed paper disc, seal and keep for up to 10 days in the fridge.

makes 800g

1 level tbsp is:

1 Syn on Extra Easy

1 Syn on Green

1 Syn on Original

ready in 1 hour 40 minutes, plus cooling

....

900g unpeeled clementines, washed

170g soft brown sugar

225ml white wine vinegar

½ tsp whole cloves

½ tsp mixed peppercorns

1 cinnamon stick

festive apple and tomato chutney

Give your cheeseboard the VIP treatment with our mouth-watering chutney.

Place all the ingredients in a large saucepan, season to taste and heat gently until the sugar has dissolved completely.

Bring to the boil over a high heat, stirring, then simmer on a low heat for 1 hour or until thick and pulpy, stirring regularly to make sure the mixture does not burn.

Leave the chutney to cool, then pour into two sterilised half-litre Kilner jars (see tip, below), cover with a waxed paper disc and seal. The chutney will keep for up to 10 days in the fridge.

You'll need two half-litre Kilner jars or similar for both of these recipes. To sterilise the jars, wash thoroughly in warm soapy water, rinse and heat in a moderate oven for 5 minutes.

makes 900g

1 level tbsp is:

½ **Syn** on Extra Easy

½ **Syn** on Green

½ **Syn** on Original

ready in 1½ hours

....

1kg ripe tomatoes, chopped

2 onions, chopped

30g sultanas or raisins

250g cooking apples, peeled, cored and chopped

50g dark brown sugar

1-2 tbsp sweetener

200ml white wine vinegar

½ tsp ground allspice

1 tsp ground ginger

1 tsp paprika

4 cloves

1 cinnamon stick

salt and freshly ground black pepper

a sweet Christmas

Our fabulously festive desserts and bakes will have everyone dreaming of a sweet Christmas.

Christmas pudding

serves 10

each serving is:

7 Syns on Extra Easy

7 Syns on Green

7 Syns on Original

ready in 8½ hours, plus soaking

225g dried mixed fruit

1 tbsp brandy

50g white self-raising flour

85g white bread, crumbed

50g dark brown sugar

170g carrots, peeled and finely grated

1 cooking apple, peeled, cored and grated

1 tsp mixed spice

½ tsp freshly grated nutmeg

a pinch of ground cinnamon

grated zest of 1 orange

grated zest of 1 unwaxed lemon

3 large eggs, beaten

75ml Guinness or stout

cranberries, to decorate

mint sprig, to decorate

1 level tsp icing sugar, to dust

Our version of the essential dessert for Christmas Day is just as fruity and tasty – and it's never been so light!

Put the dried fruit in a bowl with the brandy, mix well and leave to soak for several hours or overnight if time permits.

Add all the other ingredients to the dried fruit and brandy (remembering to make a wish!) and mix thoroughly.

Tip the mixture into a 1.2 litre pudding basin. Cover with a double thickness of baking parchment and then a piece of foil and tie securely with string.

Place the pudding on top of a steamer above gently simmering water. Cover with a lid and steam gently for 5 hours, topping up the water in the bottom of the steamer if necessary.

When the pudding is cold, replace the covers with clean ones and store in a cool, dry place until Christmas Day (it can be stored for up to 3 months).

Reheat on Christmas morning by steaming gently for 3 hours. Alternatively, remove the covers, place cling film over the basin and microwave on high for 6 minutes. Turn out on to a serving dish, decorate with cranberries and a mint sprig and dust with icing sugar to serve.

1 hour menu!

see page 6

cherry Christmas trifles

serves 4

each serving is:

3½ **Syns** on Extra Easy

3½ **Syns** on Green

3½ **Syns** on Original

ready in 15 minutes

....

200g frozen cherries, thawed

½ tsp sweetener

2 tsp cherry brandy or kirsch

1 level tbsp cherry conserve

2 soft amaretti biscuits, crushed

200g low fat custard from
a can or carton

4 tbsp fat free natural fromage frais,
sweetened to taste

fresh cherries, to decorate (or use
frozen cherries, thawed)

Our super-speedy individual trifles feature creamy custard, crunchy amaretti biscuits plus four kinds of cherry, including sweet cherry conserve and even a splash of cherry brandy. We wish you a cherry Christmas!

Put the thawed cherries in a bowl with the sweetener, cherry brandy and cherry conserve and stir to mix well.

Spoon three-quarters of the amaretti biscuit crumbs into four dessert glasses.

Divide the cherry mixture between the dessert glasses and spoon over the custard. Add a dollop of fromage frais to each glass, scatter over the reserved amaretti crumbs and decorate with a fresh cherry.

Chill until you're ready to eat.

baileys
chocolate cheesecake

serves 10

each serving is:

4 Syns on Extra Easy

4 Syns on Green

4 Syns on Original

ready in 45 minutes,
plus cooling and chilling

....

low calorie cooking spray

10 ginger biscuits

3 egg whites*

4 tsp powdered gelatine

450g quark

500g fat free natural fromage frais,
plus 4 tbsp, sweetened to taste,
to serve

4 tbsp Baileys Irish Cream liqueur

3-4 tbsp sweetener

25g chocolate curls, to decorate
(or use grated milk chocolate)

*Pregnant women, the elderly and
babies are advised not to eat raw
or partially cooked eggs.*

It's hard to say no to a slice of cheesecake at the best of times. Add the flavour of the ever-popular Christmas tipple and it's almost impossible!

Preheat the oven to 190°C/Fan 170°C/Gas 5.

Spray a 20cm spring clip cake tin with low calorie cooking spray and line with baking parchment.

Put the biscuits in a polythene bag and crush with a rolling pin.

In a bowl, lightly beat 1 egg white, add the biscuit crumbs and mix well. Press evenly over the base of the cake tin and bake for 15 minutes or until firm and golden. Leave to cool.

Dissolve the gelatine in 4 tablespoons of boiling water.

Mix the quark with the fromage frais, liqueur and sweetener. Whisk the remaining egg whites until stiff peaks form, then fold into the quark mixture along with the gelatine. Pour on to the biscuit base, smooth the top and chill for 3 hours or until set.

Release the cheesecake from the tin and pile the extra fromage frais into the middle. Crumble over the chocolate curls to decorate and slice to serve.

tropical fruit salad
with rum cream

Exotic fruits like kiwi, mango and pineapple are a refreshing and colourful way to finish a big meal, while our special rum cream brings a touch of luxury.

Scoop out the passion fruit seeds and pulp and put in a small saucepan with the sweetener and 200ml of water. Bring to the boil and cook gently for 3-4 minutes or until the sweetener has dissolved and the mixture has thickened. Set aside to cool.

Meanwhile, put the pineapple, mango, kiwi fruits, grapes, mango juice, pineapple juice, lime juice and most of the lime zest in a large serving bowl and mix well.

Make the rum cream. Spoon the fromage frais into a small serving bowl. Put the egg white in a large clean glass bowl and beat with a hand-held whisk until stiff peaks form. Fold the egg white, sweetener and rum into the fromage frais and scatter over the remaining lime zest.

Spoon the passion fruit syrup over the fruit, toss to mix well and divide between dessert glasses. Decorate the glasses with mint sprigs and serve with the rum cream.

1 hour menu!

see page 6

serves 4

each serving is:

1½ Syns on Extra Easy

1½ Syns on Green

1½ Syns on Original

Ⓥ

ready in 15 minutes

....

4 passion fruits, halved

2 tsp sweetener

100g prepared pineapple chunks

100g prepared mango chunks

3 kiwi fruits, peeled and cubed

100g seedless red and green grapes

1 tbsp mango juice

1 tbsp unsweetened pineapple juice

finely grated zest and juice of ½ unwaxed lime

mint sprigs, to decorate

for the rum cream

200g fat free natural fromage frais

1 egg white*

1 tsp sweetener

2 tbsp dark rum

Pregnant women, the elderly and babies are advised not to eat raw or partially cooked eggs.

festive semifreddo

serves 10

each serving is:

4 Syns on Extra Easy

4 Syns on Green

4 Syns on Original

ready in 15 minutes,
plus freezing

2 egg whites*

400g fat free natural
fromage frais

400g low fat custard
from a can or carton

1 tbsp sweetener

1 tsp ground ginger

1 tsp ground cinnamon

a pinch of freshly grated nutmeg

2 level tbsp mixed citrus peel

200g raspberries

300g reduced fat vanilla
ice cream, softened

1 level tsp icing sugar, to dust

*Pregnant women, the elderly and
babies are advised not to eat raw
or partially cooked eggs.*

Semifreddo means half-cold in Italian, and this beautiful blend of ice and spice is a fantastic low-Syn alternative to ice cream.

Line a large loaf tin with a double layer of cling film and line the base with non-stick baking parchment.

In a large bowl, whisk the egg whites until soft peaks form then fold in the fromage frais, custard, sweetener, spices, citrus peel, three-quarters of the raspberries and the softened ice cream. Stir to mix well and pour into the loaf tin. Cover with layers of baking parchment and then cling film and freeze for 6-8 hours or overnight.

Remove from the freezer, turn out on to a board or serving plate and leave to soften for 10 minutes. Decorate with the remaining raspberries, dust with icing sugar and slice thickly to serve.

poached clementines

Take clementines to a new level by poaching them in our seriously Christmassy spiced syrup.

Put all of the ingredients apart from the clementines and cranberries in a saucepan and bring to the boil over a high heat. Add the clementines, reduce the heat to low and simmer uncovered for 10 minutes, turning the clementines every 2 minutes. Remove the clementines with a slotted spoon and set aside to cool.

Bring the syrup back to the boil and cook over a high heat for 30 minutes, adding the cranberries for the last 8-10 minutes (the syrup should reduce by around half). Set aside to cool.

Pour the cooled syrup over the clementines and chill for 6-8 hours or overnight if time permits.

Serve the clementines in shallow bowls with the syrup spooned over.

serves 6

each serving is:

4 Syns on Extra Easy

4 Syns on Green

4 Syns on Original

Ⓥ (if the wine is vegetarian)

ready in 1 hour,
plus cooling and chilling

....

150ml light-bodied red wine
(such as merlot or beaujolais)

1 litre lemongrass tea
or raspberry tea

2 cinnamon sticks

4 whole cloves

2 star anise

6 black peppercorns

1-2 tbsp sweetener

12 clementines, peeled

200g cranberries

1 hour menu!
see page 6

boozy fruit brûlées

serves 4

each serving is:

2 Syns on Extra Easy

2 Syns on Green

2 Syns on Original

ready in 15 minutes,
plus cooling and chilling

. . . .

2 level tbsp caster sugar

2 clementines, peeled
and segmented

200g prepared mango chunks

1 tbsp brandy or Cointreau

sweetener, to taste (optional)

500g fat free natural yogurt

Our irresistibly creamy brûlées are an amazingly low-Syn version of the classic dessert, with a deliciously crunchy sugar topping to crack your spoon through!

Put the sugar in a small pan and melt over a medium heat, stirring occasionally, to make the caramel. It's ready when the sugar has completely melted and is golden in colour – this will take about 10 minutes.

Meanwhile, put the fruit into a large bowl and sprinkle over the brandy or Cointreau and sweetener, if using. Mix well and divide between four heatproof ramekins or small dishes. Spoon the yogurt over the fruit to cover and level the top of each serving.

Take the caramel off the heat. Wrap a tea towel around your hand and add a tablespoon of hot water very carefully in case it spits. Stir well and leave to cool for a minute or two, then spoon the caramel over the yogurt.

Cool and chill until you're ready to eat.

cardamom panna cottas

serves 4

each serving is:

Free on Extra Easy

Free on Green

Free on Original

ready in 20 minutes, plus chilling

....

12g gelatine sachet

200g quark

¼ tsp cardamom seeds, finely crushed

4 tbsp sweetener

1 tsp vanilla extract

2 x 175g pots Muller Light Vanilla yogurt or another Free vanilla yogurt

1 egg white*

60g pomegranate seeds, to decorate

4 vanilla pods, to decorate (optional)

Pregnant women, the elderly and babies are advised not to eat raw or partially cooked eggs.

These elegant Italian-style desserts are deliciously creamy and feature the Middle Eastern flavours of cardamom and pomegranate. Amazingly, they're Free on all choices!

Put 2 tablespoons of hot water in a small heatproof bowl and sprinkle in the gelatine. Stand the bowl in a saucepan of hot water, stir until the gelatine is dissolved and leave to cool.

Whisk the quark until smooth. Add the cardamom seeds, sweetener, vanilla extract and yogurts and whisk again until smooth. Stir in the gelatine once it has cooled.

Beat the egg white until soft peaks form and gently fold it through the yogurt mixture. Spoon the mixture into individual moulds and chill for 3-4 hours or overnight if time permits.

Dip the moulds in hot water for a few seconds and turn out the panna cottas on to serving plates.

Scatter over the pomegranate seeds and decorate with vanilla pods, if using, to serve.

If you don't like the idea of making a dessert with cardamom, larger supermarkets stock peppermint, orange, lemon and almond flavourings, which are Free and would all work well. Use 1 teaspoon instead of the cardamom, and change the pomegranate seeds for another fruit if you like.

mulled wine trifle

serves 8

each serving is:

3 Syns on Extra Easy

3 Syns on Green

3 Syns on Original

ready in 30 minutes,
plus cooling and chilling

....

8 sheets of leaf gelatine

11.5g sachet of sugar-free
raspberry jelly crystals

1cm piece of root ginger, peeled
and grated

1 cinnamon stick

1 star anise

2 cloves

6 cardamom pods

100ml red wine

1 tsp sweetener

grated zest of 1 orange

400g mixed berries,
thawed if frozen

400g low fat custard
from a can or carton

500g fat free natural fromage frais

1 tsp vanilla bean extract

1 level tsp edible gold
and silver decorations

Wobbly jelly, fresh fruit and creamy custard plus the flavours of mulled wine make this a dessert that's as festive as can be!

Put the gelatine sheets into a bowl of cold water and leave for 10-12 minutes or until softened.

Meanwhile, stir the jelly crystals into 400ml of boiling water and set aside.

Place a saucepan over a low heat and add the ginger, cinnamon stick, star anise, cloves, cardamom pods, red wine, sweetener and orange zest. Heat until hot but not boiling.

Squeeze the excess water out of the gelatine sheets and put the sheets into a large bowl.

Strain the wine mixture through a sieve on to the gelatine sheets then add the jelly mixture, stir well and leave to cool.

Put the fruit into a large glass serving bowl and pour in enough of the cooled jelly mixture to come about two-thirds of the way up the side, leaving room for the custard and fromage frais (you can use any leftover jelly mixture to make individual jellies). Chill overnight.

Spoon the custard over the jelly, then whisk together the fromage frais and vanilla and spoon on top. Scatter over the edible decorations to serve.

chocolate shots

These indulgent pots of luxury will be a big hit with the chocolate-lovers among your friends and family.

Melt the chocolate in a heatproof bowl over a pan of simmering water then leave to cool for 10 minutes.

Beat the egg yolks, sweetener and rum into the cooled chocolate. Whisk the egg whites until just stiff but not too dry then fold into the chocolate.

Transfer the mixture into small serving glasses (shot glasses are ideal) and chill for 1 hour or until set.

Top each pot with a dollop of fromage frais and decorate with chocolate sprinkles and a white chocolate star.

serves 4

each serving is:

6 Syns on Extra Easy

6 Syns on Green

6 Syns on Original

ready in 20 minutes, plus cooling and chilling

....

60g dark plain chocolate

3 eggs, separated*

3-4 tbsp sweetener

2 tbsp dark rum

4 tbsp fat free natural fromage frais, sweetened to taste

1 level tbsp chocolate sprinkles, to decorate

4 white chocolate stars, to decorate

Pregnant women, the elderly and babies are advised not to eat raw or partially cooked eggs.

star biscuits

It's great fun making and decorating these pretty biscuits… and they're perfect when you feel like a nibble.

makes 36

each biscuit is:

3 Syns on Extra Easy

3 Syns on Green

3 Syns on Original

V

ready in 45 minutes, plus cooling

a pinch of salt

1 level tsp baking powder

1 level tsp ground almonds

100g low fat margarine, suitable for baking

100g dark muscovado sugar

300g plain flour

2 large eggs, lightly beaten

4 level tbsp runny honey

25g icing sugar, made up according to packet instructions

1 level tbsp edible decorations, such as 100s and 1000s

Preheat the oven to 160°C/Fan 140°C/Gas 3.

Put the salt, baking powder, almonds, margarine and sugar in a food processor. Add the flour, reserving one teaspoon to dust, and blend well. Slowly add the eggs and honey until the mixture comes together.

Dust a work surface with the reserved flour, roll out the mixture to a 5mm thickness and cut into star shapes (or any shapes you like) using a biscuit cutter. Re-roll the trimmings and cut out more shapes until you have 36 biscuits. Arrange the stars on two baking sheets lined with baking parchment and bake for 20 minutes.

Remove from the oven, transfer to a wire rack and leave to cool.

Decorate with icing sugar and scatter over the edible decorations before serving.

We cut our biscuits into a variety of shapes and sizes so 3 Syns is an average for the biscuits shown here – if you want to make sure each biscuit is exactly 3 Syns, use one cutter for all 36.

Star Biscuits

yule log

serves 12

each serving is:

3½ Syns on Extra Easy

3½ Syns on Green

3½ Syns on Original

ready in 50 minutes, plus cooling and chilling

....

6 eggs, plus 2 yolks

85g caster sugar

60g self-raising flour

50g cocoa powder, plus 2 tsp to dust

6 sheets of leaf gelatine

150ml skimmed milk

3-4 tbsp sweetener, to taste

1 level tbsp cornflour

1 tsp coffee essence

2 tsp icing sugar, to dust

Whether you serve it as a festive dessert or a teatime treat, a Yule log is a wonderful thing to have in your kitchen over Christmas! Our recipe cuts out the double cream and chocolate traditionally used in Yule log fillings, giving you big Syn savings.

Preheat the oven to 190°C/Fan 170°C/Gas 5.

Put the six eggs and the sugar into a large mixing bowl and whisk until doubled in size.

Sieve the flour and cocoa powder into the eggs and fold in.

Line a 40cm x 30cm Swiss roll tin with baking parchment, pour in the mixture and bake for around 10 minutes or until springy to the touch. Leave to cool slightly.

While the sponge is still warm, turn it out on to a sheet of baking parchment with a damp clean tea towel underneath and gently roll it up.

Put the gelatine sheets in a bowl of cold water for 10-12 minutes or until soft.

Put the milk into a saucepan over a medium heat and heat until hot but not boiling.

Meanwhile, put the extra egg yolks into a bowl with the sweetener, cornflour and 150ml of water. Stir well and tip this mixture into the hot milk then heat gently until thickened, stirring occasionally.

Squeeze the excess liquid out of the gelatine sheets and add the sheets to the milk along with the coffee essence. Stir well, then remove from the heat and leave to cool.

Unroll the sponge and spread the mixture over it evenly. Roll up carefully and leave to set in the freezer for 3-4 hours or overnight if possible. Transfer to the fridge about an hour or two before you want to eat it.

Dust with the extra cocoa powder and icing sugar and slice to serve.

mince tarts

makes 32

each tart is:

3½ Syns on Extra Easy

3½ Syns on Green

3½ Syns on Original

ready in 45 minutes,
plus chilling and cooling

....

225g plain flour

a pinch of salt

110g butter or margarine,
cut into small cubes

low calorie cooking spray

16 level tbsp mincemeat

Nothing says Christmas like a mince tart and these beauties will be loved by friends and family alike. Standard mince pies are 12 Syns each, so you'll make a big Syn saving every time you tuck in.

Make the pastry. Sift the flour and salt into a mixing bowl, reserving 1 teaspoon of the flour for dusting, then add the butter or margarine and gently rub it in with your fingertips. Add cold water until the mixture is wet enough to mix into a ball that leaves the sides of the bowl clean. Chill for 30 minutes.

Preheat the oven to 190°C/Fan 170°C/Gas 5 and lightly spray 32 bun tin holes with low calorie cooking spray.

Sprinkle the reserved flour over a work surface then roll out the pastry thinly. Cut out 32 rounds with a 7.5cm fluted cutter and use to line the bun tin holes. Reserve the trimmings to make the pastry stars.

Divide the mincemeat between the pastry cases, using about half a tablespoon for each one.

Roll out the remaining pastry trimmings and make some little stars with a cutter. Use these to decorate the tops of the tarts.

Bake for 15 minutes or until the pastry is crisp and lightly coloured, then leave to cool on a wire rack.

Dust with a light sprinkling of icing sugar if desired (count 1 Syn per teaspoon).

leftover makeovers

Make turkey sandwiches a thing of the past with these inspiring ideas for reinventing your leftovers.

quick Christmas curry

serves 4

each serving is:

Free on Extra Easy

4 Syns on Original

10½ Syns on Green

ready in 30 minutes

....

low calorie cooking spray

1 large onion, roughly chopped

1 red pepper, halved, deseeded
and thickly sliced

1 yellow pepper, halved, deseeded
and thickly sliced

1 orange pepper, halved,
deseeded and thickly sliced

1 tbsp medium curry powder

1cm piece of root ginger,
peeled and finely grated

4 garlic cloves, crushed

400g can chopped tomatoes

200ml boiling chicken stock

500g leftover lean turkey,
skin and visible fat removed,
cut into chunks

400g leftover potatoes,
cooked without fat,
cut into chunks

salt and freshly ground
black pepper

small handful of roughly chopped
fresh coriander, plus sprigs
to garnish

Turn those turkey and potato leftovers into a Free festive fakeaway with our clever Indian-style recipe!

Spray a large non-stick frying pan with low calorie cooking spray and place over a medium-high heat. Add the onion and peppers and stir-fry for 3-4 minutes or until starting to soften and brown slightly. Stir in the curry powder, ginger and garlic, and cook for 1-2 minutes.

Add the tomatoes and stock then bring to the boil over a high heat and bubble for 5 minutes.

Turn the heat to low, stir in the turkey and potatoes and cook for 6-8 minutes.

Season to taste, scatter over the chopped coriander and garnish with the sprigs.

For extra creaminess, serve this curry with a bowl of fat free natural yogurt, sprinkled with ground cumin or cinnamon.

turkey risotto

serves 4

each serving is:

Free on Extra Easy

10½ Syns on Green

11 Syns on Original

ready in 1 hour 15 minutes

....

1 large onion, chopped

2 leeks, trimmed and chopped

1 red pepper, halved, deseeded and chopped

1 yellow pepper, halved, deseeded and chopped

2 garlic cloves, crushed

700ml boiling chicken stock

250g dried arborio rice

large pinch of saffron (or use ½ tsp turmeric)

500g leftover lean turkey, skin and visible fat removed, cut into bite-sized pieces

salt and freshly ground black pepper

small handful of finely chopped fresh parsley, to garnish

Give your leftover turkey a twist with this delicious Italian favourite.

Put the onion, leeks, peppers, garlic and 300ml of the stock in a large heavy frying pan. Cover the pan, bring to the boil over a high heat and cook for 5-10 minutes. Uncover the pan, reduce the heat to medium-low and simmer for 25 minutes or until the vegetables are tender and syrupy.

Stir in the rice and cook gently for 2 minutes, then add some more stock and the saffron (or turmeric) and bring to the boil.

Reduce the heat to a bare simmer and cook gently for 15-20 minutes, adding more stock when each ladleful of stock has been absorbed.

Add the cooked turkey after 10 minutes and heat through in the rice. The risotto is ready when the rice is plump and tender, and all the liquid has been absorbed. Season to taste and scatter over the parsley to serve.

chilli beef noodles

serves 4

each serving is:

½ Syn on Extra Easy

10½ Syns on Green

16 Syns on Original

ready in 20 minutes

....

350g dried medium egg noodles

2 tbsp light soy sauce

1 tbsp Thai fish sauce (nam pla)

1 level tbsp sweet chilli sauce

juice of ½ lime

2 red chillies, deseeded and sliced (or seeds in for extra heat)

low calorie cooking spray

bunch of spring onions, roughly chopped

400g leftover lean roast beef, visible fat removed, thinly sliced or diced

1cm piece of root ginger, peeled and finely grated

2 garlic cloves, crushed

410g can bean sprouts, drained and rinsed

225g can water chestnuts, drained, rinsed and sliced

1 carrot, peeled and cut into matchsticks

200g baby sweetcorn, halved lengthways

150g mangetout, halved lengthways

Turn the last of your Christmas joint into a sizzling Asian stir-fry!

Cook the noodles according to the pack instructions, then drain and set aside.

Meanwhile, mix the three sauces with the lime juice and most of the chilli and set aside.

Spray a large non-stick wok or frying pan with low calorie cooking spray and place over a high heat. Add the spring onions, beef, ginger, garlic, bean sprouts, water chestnuts, carrot, sweetcorn and mangetout and stir-fry for 1-2 minutes.

Add the noodles and sauce mix to the wok and stir-fry for another 1-2 minutes. Remove from the heat, scatter over the remaining chilli and serve hot.

You don't have to use beef in this sizzling stir-fry – try cooked turkey, chicken, pork, prawns or salmon too!

cheesy gammon, potato and veg bake

This simple bake is a mouth-watering way to use up your leftover gammon joint, sweet vegetables and potatoes – it's just perfect for the lazy days after Christmas.

Preheat the oven to 200°C/Fan 180°C/Gas 6.

Put the spinach in a heatproof bowl and pour over a little boiling water. Leave for a minute to wilt then tip into a colander and run under cold water. Drain and squeeze out any excess liquid then pat dry with kitchen paper.

Put the spinach, gammon, spring onions, potatoes and roasted sweet vegetables in a shallow ovenproof dish and toss to mix well.

Put the remaining ingredients in a food processor and blend until fairly smooth, then season to taste and pour over the gammon mixture. Bake for 35 minutes or until set and lightly browned.

Serve warm or at room temperature.

serves 4

each serving is:

2 Syns on Extra Easy

5½ Syns on Original

9½ Syns on Green

ready in 50 minutes

....

large bag of spinach leaves

300g leftover gammon, visible fat removed, cut into bite-sized chunks

half a bunch of spring onions, finely sliced

400g leftover potatoes, cooked without fat, cut into bite-sized chunks

200g leftover sweet vegetable roast (see page 62) or use any other Free cooked veg

small handful of fresh chives

4 eggs, lightly beaten

200g low fat natural cottage cheese

50g reduced fat Cheddar cheese, grated

2 pinches of freshly ground nutmeg

salt and freshly ground black pepper

poached salmon kedgeree

serves 4

each serving is:

Free on Extra Easy

9 Syns on Green

16½ Syns on Original

ready in 45 minutes,
plus soaking and standing

....

350g dried basmati rice

low calorie cooking spray

1 onion, finely chopped

1 large carrot, peeled and diced

1 red pepper, halved,
deseeded and diced

2 tsp cumin seeds

1-2 tbsp medium curry powder

100g frozen peas

700ml boiling fish or chicken stock

2 eggs

400g leftover poached salmon,
roughly flaked

juice of ½ lemon, plus wedges
to serve

small handful of finely chopped
fresh coriander, to garnish

The classic Anglo-Indian rice dish always goes down well – and it's a brilliant way to use up that side of salmon.

Wash the rice in a bowl of cold water and rinse under cold running water until it runs clear. Cover with cold water and leave to soak for 15-20 minutes if time permits. Drain well and set aside.

Meanwhile, spray a non-stick frying-pan (that has a tight-fitting lid) with low calorie cooking spray and place over a medium heat. Add the onion, carrot and pepper and stir-fry for 5 minutes.

Add the cumin seeds and curry powder and stir-fry for 2-3 minutes, then add the rice and peas. Cook for 1 minute, stirring, then pour in the stock.

Bring to the boil over a high heat, cover with the lid and turn the heat down to very low. Cook for 12-15 minutes then remove from the heat and leave to stand for 10-15 minutes, still covered.

At the same time, cook the eggs to your liking in a pan of boiling water (4 minutes for runny up to 10 minutes for hard-boiled) then plunge them into cold water. When the eggs are cool enough to handle, peel and halve them.

Fluff up the rice with a fork and gently fold in the fish and lemon juice. Cover for a further 2 minutes, so the salmon can heat through in the rice. Top with the boiled eggs, scatter over the coriander and serve warm with lemon wedges.

bauble and squeak cakes

These tasty cakes are an inventive way to enjoy potatoes second time around. Try them as a side dish with meat or fish, or as a lighter meal topped with fried eggs.

Preheat the oven to 200°C/Fan 180°C/Gas 6.

Put the potatoes and Brussels sprouts in a food processor with the spring onions, egg, garlic and dill. Season to taste and blend until fairly smooth.

Transfer the mixture to a bowl and knead until fairly firm. Divide the mixture into eight portions and form each one into a small cake.

Arrange the cakes on a baking sheet lined with non-stick baking parchment, spray with low calorie cooking spray and bake for 15-20 minutes or until lightly coloured, turning once.

Garnish with dill sprigs and serve hot with lemon wedges.

makes 8

each cake is:

Free on Extra Easy

Free on Green

1½ Syns on Original

ready in 30 minutes

·····································

300g leftover potatoes, cooked without fat, roughly chopped

200g leftover Brussels sprouts, roughly chopped

half a bunch of spring onions, trimmed and roughly chopped

1 egg, lightly beaten

1 garlic clove, crushed

small handful of fresh dill, plus sprigs to garnish

salt and freshly ground black pepper

low calorie cooking spray

lemon wedges, to serve

get the party started

Dazzle your friends and family with our sparkling spread of divine drinks and fully Food Optimised nibbles.

mulled wine

Nothing warms the cockles like wine infused with cloves and cinnamon.

serves 8

each serving is:

3½ Syns on Extra Easy

3½ Syns on Green

3½ Syns on Original

(V) (if the wine is vegetarian)

ready in 20 minutes

....

75cl (750ml) bottle red wine

1 tbsp brandy or rum

grated zest and juice of ½ unwaxed lemon

1 cinnamon stick, plus extra sticks to serve (optional)

2 cloves

a pinch of freshly grated nutmeg

2 level tsp brown sugar

½ orange, thinly sliced, for decoration

Pour the wine into a large saucepan. Add 300ml of water, the brandy or rum, lemon zest and juice, spices and sugar. Stir with a wooden spoon over a low heat until the wine is hot and the sugar has dissolved, taking care not to let it boil.

Transfer the wine to a heatproof jug and float the orange slices on top. Pour into heatproof glasses and serve with cinnamon sticks, if you like.

lime spritzer

Wine goes further when you spritz it up – and puts a spring in everyone's step.

serves 8

each serving is:

2 Syns on Extra Easy

2 Syns on Green

2 Syns on Original

(V) (if the wine is vegetarian)

ready in 5 minutes

....

3 limes, thinly sliced

400ml dry white wine

650ml sparkling water

3 tbsp ginger cordial

ice cubes, to serve

Put the lime slices in a large jug, stir in the white wine, sparkling water and ginger cordial and chill.

Pour into glasses and serve with ice.

Replace the ginger cordial and sparkling water with the same amount of low calorie ginger ale to save ½ Syn per serving.

festive fruit punch

This non-alcoholic punch is perfect for children, tee-totallers and designated drivers!

serves 8

each serving is:

2 Syns on Extra Easy

2 Syns on Green

2 Syns on Original

ready in 15 minutes

....

300ml unsweetened apple juice

150ml cranberry juice

150ml mango juice

500ml low calorie tonic water or soda water

250g seedless grapes (a mix of colours will look great)

ice cubes or crushed ice, to serve

....

Chill all the fruit juices and the tonic or soda water in the fridge.

Thread the grapes on to eight cocktail sticks and set aside.

Pour the fruit juices and the tonic or soda water into a large jug, stir well and add plenty of ice. Pour the punch into glasses and top each one with a grape stick to serve.

beef kofte with a creamy tomato dip

makes 30

each kofte is:

Free on Extra Easy

Free on Original

2 Syns on Green

❄ (without the dip)

ready in 25 minutes

....

1kg lean beef mince
(5% fat or less)

3 garlic cloves, crushed

½ red onion, finely chopped

2 tsp medium curry powder

small handful of finely
chopped fresh mint

30 fresh rosemary sprigs
or cocktail sticks

for the tomato dip

200g fat free natural
fromage frais

100g passata

salt and freshly ground
black pepper

Our spectacular spiced Middle Eastern meatballs are skewered on rosemary sprig cocktail sticks to guarantee your party spread has the wow factor!

Preheat the grill to medium.

Make the dip by putting the fromage frais and passata in a small bowl. Season and mix well then cover and chill until you're ready to serve.

Put the beef in a large bowl with the garlic, red onion, curry powder and mint. Mix to combine using your hands.

Divide the mixture into 30 portions, shape each one into a ball and spread them out on the grill pan. Grill for around 10 minutes or until cooked through, turning occasionally.

Skewer each kofte with a rosemary sprig, arrange on a platter and serve with the chilled dip.

spicy spuds

Everyone loves roast potatoes and these hot and spicy spuds are perfect for a party.

Preheat the oven to 220°C/Fan 200°C/Gas 7.

Place the potatoes in a non-stick roasting tin in a single layer.

Mix the spices and passata in a bowl, season to taste and pour over the potatoes. Toss to coat evenly.

Spray with low calorie cooking spray and roast for 45-50 minutes or until tender.

Remove the potatoes from the oven, pile them into a serving bowl and scatter over most of the dried coriander.

Sprinkle the remaining dried coriander over a bowl of fat free natural yogurt and serve with the potatoes.

makes 48 halves

each half is:

Free on Extra Easy

Free on Green

½ **Syn** on Original

ready in 1 hour

....

24 baby new potatoes, washed and halved

2 tsp paprika

2 tsp dried chilli flakes

2 tsp cumin seeds

2 tsp black onion seeds

120g passata

salt and freshly ground black pepper

low calorie cooking spray

1 tbsp dried coriander, to garnish

fat free natural yogurt, to serve

mozzarella cups

We've filled irresistible filo pastry with juicy peppers and creamy mozzarella to make these indulgent bites.

Preheat the oven to 180°C/Fan 160°C/Gas 4.

Spray the pastry with low calorie cooking spray. Using a sharp knife, cut the pastry into 5cm x 5cm pieces.

Spray a mini muffin tin with low calorie cooking spray and line 24 holes with a square of pastry. Spray with low calorie cooking spray and lay the rest of the pastry squares on top of the first ones at slightly different angles. Bake for 6-8 minutes or until brown, then transfer to a wire rack to cool.

Meanwhile, mix the mozzarella, peppers and basil in a bowl.

Once the filo cups have cooled, fill with the mozzarella mixture and scatter over the basil leaves to serve.

makes 24 cups

each cup is:

1 Syn on Extra Easy

1 Syn on Green

1 Syn on Original

Ⓥ

ready in 30 minutes, plus cooling

2 x 45g sheets ready-rolled filo pastry

low calorie cooking spray

150g reduced fat mozzarella, drained and roughly chopped

2 bottled roasted red peppers in brine, drained and roughly chopped

small handful of finely chopped fresh basil, plus small leaves to garnish

turkey tikka skewers

makes 12

each skewer is:

Free on Extra Easy

Free on Original

3½ Syns on Green

ready in 30 minutes, plus marinating

....

200g fat free natural yogurt, plus extra to serve

3 tbsp tikka or tandoori curry powder, plus extra to serve

3 garlic cloves, finely grated

3cm piece of root ginger, peeled and finely grated

juice of 2 limes, plus wedges to serve

salt and freshly ground black pepper

800g turkey breast fillets, cut into bite-sized pieces

2 red peppers, halved, deseeded and cut into bite-sized pieces

small handful of finely chopped fresh coriander, to garnish

Give Christmas turkey a tasty twist with these more-ish Indian skewers.

Mix the yogurt, tikka or tandoori powder, garlic, ginger and lime juice in a large bowl. Season to taste, add the turkey and stir to coat well. Cover and marinate in the fridge for 20 minutes or overnight if time permits.

Preheat the grill to medium-hot.

Thread the turkey chunks and peppers on to 12 metal skewers (or wooden skewers soaked in water for 20 minutes to stop them burning). Grill for 6-8 minutes on each side or until the edges are lightly charred in places and the turkey is cooked through.

Arrange the skewers on a serving platter, scatter over the coriander and serve hot with lime wedges and a bowl of fat free natural yogurt sprinkled with tikka or tandoori curry powder.

You can make these stunning skewers with chunks of skinless chicken breast if you prefer.

Make the party Last

double salmon and cucumber bombe

This stylish party centrepiece looks amazing and tastes even better – so ask your guests to form an orderly queue!

Put the salmon fillets, bay leaf, peppercorns and onion in a wide saucepan and pour in enough boiling water to just cover. Bring to the boil, cover the pan, reduce the heat to low and simmer for 8-10 minutes or until just cooked through. Lift the fish from the pan with a slotted spoon and drain on kitchen paper. Discard the bay leaf, peppercorns and onion.

Meanwhile, soak the gelatine sheets in a bowl of cold water for 10-12 minutes or until softened.

Line a 1 litre pudding basin with cling film then line the basin again with overlapping slices of the smoked salmon.

Flake the salmon fillets into a food processor and add the quark, soft cheese, dill, chives and lime zest and juice. Season to taste.

Squeeze the liquid from the gelatine sheets and add the sheets to the boiling stock, discarding the soaking water. Stir to dissolve completely and pour the stock into the food processor. Process until well blended, stir through the cucumber and leave to cool.

Pour the cheese mixture into the prepared mould, cover with cling film and chill for 6-8 hours or until set.

Carefully turn out the mould from the pudding basin and peel away the cling film. Garnish with cucumber ribbons and dill sprigs to serve.

serves 8

each serving is:

1½ Syns on Extra Easy

1½ Syns on Original

13½ Syns on Green

ready in 30 minutes, plus cooling and chilling

....

4 skinless salmon fillets

1 bay leaf

8 black peppercorns

1 onion, cut into wedges

10 sheets of leaf gelatine

500g smoked salmon

200g quark

200g extra-light soft cheese

large handful of fresh dill, plus sprigs to garnish

large handful of fresh chives

finely grated zest and juice of 1 unwaxed lime

salt and freshly ground black pepper

200ml boiling fish or chicken stock

½ cucumber, halved, deseeded and diced, plus a few thin ribbons to garnish

prawn and chilli ginger cakes

These Asian-inspired bites are packed with flavour and a warming hint of chilli. Increase the amount of chilli if you want a roaring fire for the tastebuds!

Put the bread in a food processor with the prawns, chilli, ginger, coriander and egg. Season to taste and whizz until combined. Transfer the mixture to a bowl.

Spray a non-stick frying pan with low calorie cooking spray and place over a medium heat. Using your hands, form the prawn mixture into 12 small cakes and cook in batches for 3 minutes on each side or until golden.

Garnish with mint leaves and serve hot with lemon wedges.

makes 12

each cake is:

½ **Syn** on Extra Easy

½ **Syn** on Original

1½ **Syns** on Green

ready in 30 minutes

....

4 slices of bread from a small 400g wholemeal loaf, crusts removed

250g raw peeled prawns

1 red chilli, deseeded and thinly sliced

3cm piece of root ginger, peeled and finely chopped

1 tbsp chopped fresh coriander

1 egg

salt and freshly ground black pepper

low calorie cooking spray

fresh mint leaves, to garnish

lemon wedges, to serve

cheesy bites

makes 24

each bite is:

½ **Syn** on Extra Easy

½ **Syn** on Green

½ **Syn** on Original

ready in 15 minutes

· ·

6 small ripe tomatoes

4 thick celery sticks, trimmed

5 tbsp quark

125g extra-light soft cheese

1 level tbsp reduced fat green pesto

small handful of finely chopped fresh basil

salt and freshly ground black pepper

small handful of roughly chopped fresh chives, to garnish

Halved tomatoes and crisp chunks of celery get a creamy, pesto-infused topping for these mouth-watering nibbles.

Halve the tomatoes and scoop out and discard the seeds. Cut each celery stick into three pieces.

In a bowl, mix the quark, soft cheese, pesto and basil and season to taste.

Fill the tomatoes and celery pieces with the cheese mixture and garnish with the chives to serve.

Mexican chilli beans

A big bowl of spiced beans makes great party food and our selection of tempting toppings will have your guests flocking around the table!

Spray a large non-stick frying pan with low calorie cooking spray and place over a medium heat. Add the red onions and garlic and stir-fry for 2-3 minutes. Add the smoked paprika, cinnamon and cumin and stir-fry for 8-10 minutes.

Add the tomatoes, peppers and sweetener and bring to the boil over a high heat. Season to taste, cover tightly and turn the heat to low. Cook over a low heat for 20-30 minutes, stirring occasionally.

Add the beans to the pan and stir to mix well. Cook for another 10 minutes then remove from the heat, transfer to a serving bowl and sprinkle over the coriander and extra paprika.

Put the beans, lime wedges and all the toppings on the table and invite your guests to help themselves!

serves 10

each serving is:

Free on Extra Easy

Free on Green

5½ Syns on Original

ready in 1 hour

....

low calorie cooking spray

3 red onions, finely chopped

4 garlic cloves, finely chopped

2 tsp sweet smoked paprika, plus extra to sprinkle

1 tsp ground cinnamon

1 tbsp ground cumin

2 x 400g cans chopped tomatoes

1 red pepper, halved, deseeded and diced

1 yellow pepper, halved, deseeded and diced

¼ tsp sweetener

salt and freshly ground black pepper

2 x 400g cans red kidney beans in chilli sauce

2 x 380g cartons black beans, drained (or use any canned beans)

large handful of roughly chopped fresh coriander

6 limes, cut into wedges

for the toppings

bunch of spring onions, thinly sliced

1 cucumber, finely chopped

10 red radishes, thinly sliced

500g fat free natural yogurt, sprinkled with smoked paprika

cook's tips

eggs

Pregnant women, the elderly and babies shouldn't eat raw or partially cooked eggs. We'll make a note in any recipes where raw or partially cooked eggs are used.

fat free natural fromage frais and yogurt

These are wonderful ingredients when you're Food Optimising as they give the creamy texture and taste normally achieved with cream. However, they tend to separate when boiled and can make the dish look unappetising. So unless the recipe says otherwise, add yogurt or fromage frais off the heat once all the other ingredients have been cooked and simply heat through. Both make great savoury or sweet ingredients – if you're using them to top a pudding, add sweetener and maybe some vanilla essence as well, to taste.

fresh, canned and frozen

Frozen ingredients and canned veg and beans are great alternatives to fresh foods and are so handy to keep in the cupboard or freezer. They'll keep for much longer, can be quicker to cook and are just as good for you. So feel free to switch between all three – bear in mind cooking times may change slightly.

fresh herbs

These lose their freshness quickly so if you have more than you can use, freeze them in a little water in ice cube trays – then you can add them straight to stews and curries.

fruit

While most fresh whole fruit is Free, puréed or cooked fruit counts as Syns because it isn't as filling and becomes much easier to over-consume. You'll see that in any recipes where fruit is puréed or cooked, we've counted it as Syns.

low calorie cooking spray

To cut down on fat in recipes, we recommend using non-stick cookware/bakeware wherever possible. However, if you do need to use fat then choose a low calorie cooking spray which contains 1 calorie or less per spray, as these are Free – others would need to be counted as Syns. Ideal for Christmas roast potatoes or fried eggs and Slimming World chips with roast gammon.

meat and poultry

Trim off any visible fat before cooking to make lean meat or poultry Free on Extra Easy and Original, plus remember to remove the skin before or after cooking poultry. If you cook poultry with the skin on, cook it separately from the other ingredients so that the fat can't run into them (eg potatoes roasted in the same tin).

measurements

Syns for some ingredients are based on level teaspoons or tablespoons. Without measuring carefully, it's easy to far exceed your intended Syn intake without realising – so scrape a knife along the top of the spoon, knocking the excess back into the container. For best results, invest in a set of measuring spoons.

minced meat

Lean minced meat (5% fat or less) is a Free Food on Extra Easy and Original. Beef, pork and turkey mince are available in most major supermarkets at 5% fat or less – check the nutrition information to be sure. If possible, drain off any fat that comes from the mince while you're cooking it. No chicken and lamb mince is widely available with 5% fat or less so these would have a Syn value… unless you know a friendly butcher who'll mince skinless chicken breasts or lean lamb with all visible fat removed for you.

mustard powder

Made-up mustard in jars has Syns while mustard powder is Free, making it a great choice for dressings and sauces.

salt and freshly ground black pepper

Where salt and pepper are used, we usually suggest seasoning to taste. Official advice is that adults should eat no more than 6g of salt a day – and bear in mind that small amounts can quickly add up.

stock

Fresh stock, stock cubes, stock pots, bouillon powder, ready-to-use liquid stock and liquid stock concentrate are all Free but be aware that gravy granules or powder and stock granules are not. Stock should normally be boiling when you add it to the pan, as cold stock will slow down cooking times.

symbol *sense*

ready in…

This gives a guide to how long the recipe will take to prepare and cook.

serves…

This gives you an idea of how many people the recipe can serve. However, feel free to split the recipe between more or fewer people instead, depending on how hungry you are – especially when it's Free!

freezer-friendly ❄

Recipes showing this symbol can be safely frozen for up to 1 month. Keep in mind official advice on freezing safely:

● Label food for the freezer with details of what the meal is and when you cooked it.

● Make sure food has cooled before you put it in the freezer.

● Defrost frozen meals completely and reheat thoroughly before eating.

Batch cooking: Wherever you see the freezer-friendly symbol ❄, you can save time and effort by cooking double or triple amounts and freezing the rest to enjoy at a later date. You'll usually save money too because it's often cheaper to buy ingredients in bulk.

suitable for vegetarians ⓥ

Recipes marked with this symbol are suitable for vegetarians. Recipes that contain meat, fish or poultry can often be made vegetarian by using Quorn mince or pieces, textured vegetable protein/ soya protein or tofu instead. Some ingredients that are unsuitable for vegetarians might surprise you – eg Parmesan, Worcestershire sauce, gelatine and Muller Light yogurts – although you can usually find a vegetarian alternative. It's always best to check the packaging to be sure.